YOUR KNOWLEDGE HAS VALUE

Films in the 'anti-Fascist' German Democratic Republic. The DEFA and the Memory of World War II

Christopher Borns

Bibliographic information published by the German National Library:

The German National Library lists this publication in the National Bibliography; detailed bibliographic data are available on the Internet at http://dnb.dnb.de.

ISBN: 9783346347718
This book is also available as an ebook.

© GRIN Publishing GmbH
Nymphenburger Straße 86
80636 München

Print and binding: Books on Demand GmbH, Norderstedt, Germany
Printed on acid-free paper from responsible sources.

The present work has been carefully prepared. Nevertheless, authors and publishers do not incur liability for the correctness of information, notes, links and advice as well as any printing errors.

GRIN web shop: https://www.grin.com/document/987879

SUNY Potsdam College
History Department
Student: Christopher Borns

Fall 2009

Films in the 'anti-Fascist' German Democratic Republic

What role(s) did the memory of World War II play in the construction of the GDR as the 'anti-Fascist' German state?

How did film makers in the former German Democratic Republic conceptualize, frame and display their version of World War II and its meanings?

Table of Contents

1. Introduction

Berlin, 9th of November 2009. Hundreds of people celebrated 20 years of the fall of the wall, which finally ended the Cold War between the United States of America and the Soviet Union. The war started immediately after World War II and both superpowers tried to push through their ideologies among the people all over the world, especially in Europe. Whereas the United States favored a capitalist ideology, the Soviet Union preferred a communist ideology. The struggle between them led to a significant change in Germany in 1949, namely the establishment of two German states – the (communist) German Democratic Republic (GDR) and the (capitalist) Federal Republic of Germany (FRG).

Both countries tried to strengthen their ideological positions respectively by using certain means, e.g. propaganda. Above all, the GDR regime continued using propagandistic means within the following decades to influence its population indirectly in different aspects of life, for instance in physical education[1].

During the process of the development in East and West Germany, the issue of the memory of World War II and the Nazi Past was discussed. Therefore, the GDR film institution DEFA was one of the first establishments which mainly published films shortly after 1945 to memorize the Second World War and the cruelties of the Nazis. *But how important was the role of the memory of World War II for the GDR regime in reality? And would the GDR regime also try to use propaganda in films of such a sensible and important matter? Would it also try to*

---

[1] Concerning the topic 'Propaganda in physical education' I have written a paper which analyses articles of the GDR magazine 'Körpererziehung' between 1952 and 1955. It confirms that the GDR regime used the magazine to influence its readers politically.

spread its ideology within these movies? And if, how were ideological means implied in the movies respectively how did film makers conceptualize, frame and display their versions of World War II and its meanings?

To answer these questions the paper starts by giving an overview of the importance of the memory of World War II and the Nazi Past in GDR policy. After that, this policy should be further analyzed with the help of nine movies of GDR film makers and their contribution to the memory of World War II and the Nazi Past in East Germany. The conclusion is the last part of the paper. It is pointed out to the reader of this paper that the whole topic as well as the films cannot be fully analyzed because of limited space of this paper. Therefore this paper cannot be declared as complete.

2. The Memory of the Nazi-Past in the German Democratic Republic

After the end of World War II the successful allies France, Great Britain, the United States of America and the Soviet Union divided up Germany into different occupation zones. They all had in common to destroy any form of Nazism as a political issue. The Nuremberg interregnum and following imprisonments as well as death penalties for former Nazi war criminals were helpful measures.[2] The goal to force Nazism out of politics was also held up after the establishment of the two German states out of the occupation zones – the communist orientated GDR out of

---

[2] Jeffrey Herf, *Divided Memory: The Nazi Past in the Two Germanys* (Cambridge, MA: Harvard University Press, 1997) 373.

the Soviet zone and the capitalistic orientated FRG out of the U.S., French and British zone.[3]

Both countries similarly rested their postwar memories "on interpretations of Nazism which its German opponents had begun to develop in the Weimar Republic"[4]. But the two states interpreted the meaning of 'opponents' of the Nazis dissimilarly because of their different ideologies. The leaders of the GDR favored former socialists of the Weimar Republic as the major enemies of the Nazis, while the FRG officials tended more to the democratic views of Social Democrats of the Weimar Republic.[5]

A more striking difference between both countries concerning postwar memory was the issue of the Jews and the Holocaust. Many people thought that the GDR and the Jews could find a certain basis after the Second World War for various reasons. Firstly, the Jewish and Soviet population suffered a lot from Nazi cruelties in World War II according to death numbers. Secondly, it was therefore assumed that the Soviet influenced GDR would follow an 'anti-Fascist' policy in the future and could be a home for the Jews, as well. Thirdly, the Soviet Union supported the new state of Israel, which also led to the assumption that within the Eastern part of Europe there could be a place for the Jews.[6] Nevertheless reality looked different. The Soviet officials considered their suffering and ordeals of the Second World War more important than the fate of the Jewish population.[7] Furthermore many Jews

---

[3] Ibid, 4.
[4] Ibid, 5.
[5] Ibid, 376.
[6] Ibid, 5.
[7] Ibid, 381.

were afraid of living in the GDR because it was influenced by a dictatorial Soviet Union and reminded many of the dictatorial Nazi state.[8] Moreover, "East German leaders kept the Jewish question on the margin of narratives of the Nazi era, refused to pay restitution to Jewish survivors or to Israel, purged those Communist[s] who sought to give it greater prominence and even gave [...] support to Israel's armed adversaries"[9]. Above all the marginalization of the Jews equaled the position of communists before 1933, which emphasizes that the GDR officials also rested their attitude towards Jews on interpretations of traditional communist leaders, e.g. Karl Marx. Herf states that "[i]t is striking how little [...] World War II and the Holocaust changed these long-held views"[10].

In contrast to that was the opinion of the FRG officials like Kurt Schumacher. According to them anti-Semitism could be overcome and the Holocaust would be the core of memory of the Nazi Past in both German countries.[11]

The different opinions of the officials of both countries towards such a highly sensible topic as the memory of the Holocaust and World War II illustrate that the upcoming Cold War gained more and more influence and therefore international politics and national interests played an important role in the memory of the Nazi past.[12] Especially in the GDR the memory of the Nazi past was used to legitimize the states position[13] respectively to weaken the position of the 'ideological' opponent in the West and to cover its own weaknesses (in other areas). "So

---

[8] Ibid, 5.
[9] Ibid, 3.
[10] Ibid, 376.
[11] Ibid, 378.
[12] Ibid, 383-384.
[13] Ibid, 388.

entwickelte sich in der DDR ein widersprüchlicher Antifaschismus: einerseits war

er ehrliche Überzeugung, mehrheitlich akzeptierter gesellschaftlicher

Grundkonsens und integrative Faktor, der Erziehung Schule öffentliches Leben

durchdrang, andererseits wurde er von der SED[...] mißbraucht [...]."[14] That is the

reason why the term of an 'anti-Fascist' state, which the GDR regime often used

itself, has to be viewed very critically.

Naturally, the GDR officials wanted to uphold their position among the

people and therefore used various means to reach their goal. One of these means

was the film production. Therefore on the Third Party Congress of the Socialist

Unity Party (SED) "the political function of film as an instrument of propaganda in

the service of current political activities was clearly formulated"[15]. Furthermore on

the 1st of January 1953 the DEFA, which was founded in 1946, was nationalized by

the East German government.[16] This makes obvious how the GDR could spread

their propaganda (of the SED view of history) in the film industry, strengthen their

political ideology as well as fortify the acceptance of the SED among the people.[17]

Most importantly for film productions at that time was the dealing with the

question of guilt during the Nazi time, i.e. the films showed those who were guilty

of Nazi crimes and those who fought against it. According to that the people who

---

[14] Kurt Finker, *Zwischen Integration und Legitimation: Der antifaschistische Widerstandskampf in Geschichtsbild und Geschichtsschreibung der DDR* (Schkeuditz: GNN Verlag, 1999), 170.
[15] Christiane Mückenberger, "The Anti-Fascist Past in DEFA Films" in "DEFA: East German Cinema 1946-1992" [http://books.google.com/books?id=3xDwYDJlklkC&printsec=frontcover&dq=DEFA&hl=de&cd=1#v=onepage&q=&f=false] December 1, 2009, 66.
[16] Daniela Berghan, "Hollywood behind the Wall: The cinema of East Germany" [http://books.google.com/books?id=JAr2pv4R6kIC&printsec=frontcover&dq=hollywood+behind+the+wall&hl=de&cd=1#v=onepage&q=&f=false] December 1, 2009, 19.
[17] Susanne Brandt, "Geschichte und Film: Der Untertan (1951)" [www.phil-fak.uni-duesseldorf.de/.../Der_Untertan_Geschichte_und_Film_kurz_.pdf] December 1, 2009, 10.

fought against the Nazis were socialists whereas the guilty people were naturally anti-socialists.[18] After Stalin's death in 1953 the situation for the film makers got better in terms of restricted content, but only five years later the SED took over control again.[19] At the same time more and more households got television, which made it possible for the people to watch West German television, too. This led to a decrease of viewing numbers in cinemas[20]. But GDR film makers used new visual techniques as well as more complex stories at the beginning of the 1960's which made movies more interesting and innovative. These modern sometimes system critical features did not last for long because in 1965 the GDR regime tightened up its control towards films and film makers. From then on film makers focused on less contentious issues, e.g. historical films.

In conclusion one can say that the memory of the Nazi Past was highly important for the GDR regime, but because of the emergent Cold War it was more and more used for propagandistic purposes, which apparently affected the film industry.

3. Analysis of 'Anti-Fascist' Films of German Democratic Republic Film Makers

How the affected film makers put the ideological and propagandistic demands into practice should be showed in this chapter. It should be considered that only some aspects of each film can be analyzed because of limited space of the paper.

---

[18] Mückenberger, "The Anti-Fascist Past in DEFA Films", 66.
[19] Marc Silberman, "German Cinema: Texts in Context" [http://books.google.com/books?id=xzf byafOb4QC&printsec=frontcover&dq=German+cinema&hl=de&cd=2#v=onepage&q=&f=false] December 1, 2009, 147.
[20] Susanne Brandt, "Geschichte und Film", 10-11.

3.1 The Blum Affair (1948)

Although in 1948 the GDR was not officially founded, the movie was produced in the DEFA studios which were in the Soviet zone of occupation at that time. Therefore it can be rather recognized as a GDR film because the policy of the Soviet Union and the GDR was basically the same. The movie which was directed by Erich Engel deals with anti-Semitism as well as nationalism during the Weimar Republic and is based on an actual event which took place in Magdeburg in 1926.[21]

Karl Heinz Gabler, a former soldier and thief, needs money and murders a man, called Wilhelm Platzer, and so he gets some money in form of checks. When Gabler uses them he is arrested by the police, but invents a story to acquit himself. Instead he accuses the boss of Wilhelm Platzer who is the rich Jewish manufacturer Dr. Jacob Blum. The police officer Schwerdtfeger as well as the State Prosecutor Konrat tend to believe his story because both think that Jews want to work together with left wing politicians to control the German government. That is the reason why Blum is arrested and has to stay in prison and is denied any form of contact to his wife. She believes in his innocence and asks the democratic 'Regierungspräsidenten' for help. He demands a police officer to investigate the case independently. He proves the innocence of Dr. Jacob Blum and police officer and Schwerdtfeger the State Prosecutor Konrat are embarrassed because of the mistake. The film ends by showing Blum and his wife. She says that she knew that

---

[21] DEFA Film Library at the University of Massachusetts Amherst, "Affaire Blum (The Blum Affair)" [http://www.umass.edu/defa/filmtour/sjblum.shtml] October 22, 2009, unpaginated.

everything will be clarified because they live in the German state under the rule of law, but her husband makes no reply to it.[22]

The movie perfectly fits in the category of movies dealing with the question of guilt, which was highly supported by the later GDR regime. The anti-socialist respectively conservative police officer and state Prosecutor are the ones who opposed Jews and were not interested in giving the Jews and the left wing politicians more power. In contrast to that is the more left wing Regierungspräsident who permanently tries to prove the innocence of the Jew Dr. Blum, i.e. he fights for the Jews. Thus this emphasizes that the left wing/ socialist politicians were the ones who fought for the Jews in the Weimar Republic, which makes the viewer believe that they also would fight for them in future. Therefore the communist system can be seen as a system of justice, which naturally strengthens the Soviet legitimacy.

Additionally Soviet officials censored parts of the film and gave advices to the film makers how certain persons should be depicted. Thus Major Simowski, the film censor of the Soviet Occupation Authority (SMAD), said that the character of Dr. Blum should be less portrayed as an industrial but more portrayed as a socialist fighter in the class struggle.[23] This makes obvious that the movie was strongly influenced by Soviet propaganda respectively ideology. By fitting the characters to Soviet politics, the viewer would be secretly influenced and would not immediately recognize the Soviet propaganda, because no communist signs or symbols were used but just the behavior and acting of a person.

---

[22] Ibid, unpaginated.
[23] Ibid, unpaginated.

3.2 Rotation (1949)

The first 'anti-Fascist' film of the GDR was directed by Wolfgang Staudte in 1949. It shows how blue collar workers in Germany were seduced by the Nazis and therefore did not question the negative side of the dictatorial regime.[24]

Hans Behnke, a locksmith, is one of those blue-collar people. During the final days of the Weimar Republic and the first time of the Nazi regime he becomes unemployed and has to live in very poor conditions. His entire life is based on his wife and his new born child Helmut. He gets a job in a printing company which publishes Nazi propaganda material what his brother-in-law does not like because he has joined the Communist party. Behnke stays apolitical and firstly refuses to join the Nazi Party but later on enters the party in favor of his family. In the meantime his brother-in-law has to flee but comes back after a while. He asks Hans to help him distributing resisting pamphlets. Hans agrees to help him but keeps some of the pamphlets hidden in his apartment. When his son Helmut finds them he reports to Nazi officials because he had joined the Hitler Youth. As a result Hans is arrested. After the war father and son reunite and have feelings of guilt to each other. Finally Hans demands his son to oppose Nazism in the future.[25]

As the Blum Affair this movie also fits in the category of movies about the question of guilt, which were demanded from the GDR regime. The main character is the guilty person without knowing that he supports a terrible regime respectively

---

[24] DEFA Film Library at the University of Massachusetts Amherst, "Rotation" [http://www.umass.edu/defa/filmtour/sjrotation.shtml] October 22, 2009, unpaginated.
[25] Michael Buening, "Cautionary Tales" [http://www.popmatters.com/pm/review/council-of-the-gods-der-rat-der-g/] October 22, 2009, unpaginated.

that he is guilty himself. Many viewers of the film could have seen similarities to their own situation during the Nazi era and therefore the movie emphasizes a certain effect to the viewer.[26]

Furthermore the director also introduces "a character who would become the model for future East films on anti-fascism: Hans' brother in law, the communist resistance fighter"[27]. Although he is not a main character of the movie he is depicted as the one who foresees the cruelties and crimes of the Nazis and tries Hans to join the resistance movement. Naturally such a character in a film saves ideological ideas of the GDR and influences the viewers thinking that he believes that the Nazi resistance was almost totally conducted by communists. Moreover the implementation of a communist character also had the effect that the communists had a higher morale than other Germans; that a communist society as the GDR society was, is automatically anti-fascist; that the cruelties of the Nazis were predictable – naturally by the communists.[28]

Another point which really shows that communist propaganda played an important role concerns the end of the film. Soviet officials asked Staudte to change the end of the film prior to its release. Their problem was the scene when Hans originally says to his son that he will never wear a uniform in the future again. They disliked the pacifist ending because they were establishing the 'Volkspolizei' (GDR police force) and that a pacifist element was not the mean to recruit officers for the police.

---

[26] Ibid, unpaginated.
[27] DEFA Film Library at the University of Massachusetts Amherst, "Rotation", unpaginated.
[28] Ibid, unpaginated.

Therefore the original intention of Staudte was replaced by a dictated demand of the GDR regime, which underlines the ideological and propagandistic influence of the regime in anti-fascist movies.

3.3 Council of Gods (1950)

The film was directed by Kurt Maetzig and is based on a true story of the I.G. Farben industrial company, which helped Hitler produce gas for the gas chambers in Nazi concentration camps. It deals with scientists who contributed (unknowingly) to the Nazi crimes in the concentration camps as well as with opportunistic business leaders who only want to make profit during World War II and its aftermath.[29]

A group of factory owners who call themselves 'council of gods' just want to make as much money as possible with their chemical factory, which is located in the Rhineland, during the approaching Second World War. In their factory the young Dr. Hans Scholz works as a researcher. He develops toxic gases which are used to provide the gas chambers of the concentration camp but the researcher thinks that the gases are only used to develop pesticides as well as rejects beliefs that his work is abused to kill people when he finds canisters which are labeled for the chambers of Auschwitz.

After World War II the factory owners as well as Dr. Scholz are accused of murder. Although Dr. Scholz admits partial responsibility, he and all the other industrials are punished slightly. Therefore the factory owners continue to produce

---

[29] DEFA Film Library at the University of Massachusetts Amherst, "Rat der Götter (Council of Gods" [http://www.umass.edu/defa/filmtour/sjrat.shtml] October 22, 2009, unpaginated.

chemical weapons for other wars, but this time Dr. Scholz fights against them and is supported by his co-worker Karl. Finally, the factory explodes because of the chemical weapons and Dr. Scholz publicly accuses the chairman of the council of gods, Mauch, that he only wants to make profit, regardless if people are killed or not.[30]

This film is a typical example of how the GDR regime influenced the film makers respectively the film industry to spread their ideology. The film also fits in the category of question of guilt because the more innocent (socialist) people fought against the cruelties of the Nazis and the guilty persons were the factory owners. Furthermore the latter can be seen as the bourgeoisie according to the communist ideology. So it emphasizes that the viewer should think that the bourgeoisie also was guilty of Nazi crimes and should be therefore even more opposed. Additionally, the movie was produced just one year after the 'anti-Fascist' film *Rotation* which "shows how quickly DEFA's demands to toe the party line obscured critical sentiments"[31].

Moreover the depiction of the American Standard Oil Company is obviously Anti-American. After World War II the U.S. Company enters into negotiations with the council to fight a war against the Soviets. Thus the reader should assume that the Americans do not care about working together with former Nazi criminals respectively the they also make a 'pact with the devil' only to weaken the Soviets. Thus the Soviets could strengthen their position among the people that they did not pact with the devil and that they are the only ones who can be seen as anti-Fascists.

---

[30] Ibid, unpaginated.
[31] Michael Buening, "Cautionary Tales", unpaginated.

Furthermore an actual event which took place in 1948 also played an important role for the film. In that year an explosion in a BASF factory in Ludwigshafen killed almost 300 people. Because the town was in the U.S. occupation zone the GDR regime was interested to put this event in the film and to publish the film as fast as possible.[32] Thus this emphasizes that the GDR regime tried to weaken the Western countries as much as possible to strengthen their position and also put Cold War issues in 'anti-Fascist' movies.

As in *Rotation* this film also contains a communist character in persona of Karl. He also tries to resist the factory owners and their policy. This shows that the film makers really were aware of the fact to incorporate regime friendly characters to display the communists as the 'good' unique people who fought against the evil Nazis. The effects of such a role model are the same in this film as in *Rotation*.[33]

3.4 The Axe of Wandsbek (1951)

The film deals with ordinary people at the beginning of the Nazi era, who supported the dictatorship because of personal problems but were therefore not widely accepted among the common society. The story based on the Novel of the same name, written by Arnold Zweig in 1943. The director of the film was Falk Harnack, who was a former member of the resistance group 'Weisse Rose'. His brother and his sister-in-law, also members of a resistance group, were killed by the Nazis.[34]

---

[32] DEFA Film Library at the University of Massachusetts Amherst, "Rat der Götter (Council of Gods)", unpaginated.
[33] DEFA Film Library at the University of Massachusetts Amherst, "Rotation", unpaginated.
[34] DEFA Film Library at the University of Massachusetts Amherst, "Das Beil von Wandsbek (The Axt of Wandsbek)" [http://www.umass.edu/defa/filmtour/sjaxe.shtml] October 22, 2009, unpaginated.

The butcher Albert Teetjen and his wife Stine are worried about their shop because the customers prefer modern shopping malls for buying their meat and therefore the Teetjens' do not earn so much money. Thus Stine thrusts her husband to contact his former war comrade Footh, who became a successful ship-owner, to get a job. Footh offers him 2000 Mark when Teetjen kills four communists, therefore the 'Führer' can come to Hamburg. Although Teetjens has some doubts he agrees to it and kills (beheads) the four communists. When the customers get to know that he had killed them, his financial situation got even worse. Finally, his wife commits suicide and he does the same after he had found her.[35]

The conflict between the capitalist West and the communist East also concerned this memorial 'anti-Fascist' movie of the DEFA. The GDR officials banned the movie after few days because they argued that the viewer would feel pity with the main character and not focuses on the crime he did. Thus the Nazis crimes could be more a mistake of an individual than of a fascist dictatorial regime.[36] This illustrates that the GDR officials feared to lose their self-given status of an 'anti-Fascist' state, which was part of the legitimacy. According to the directors past this ban was naturally not logical but the regime probably focused on not making a mistake that could be used by the ideological opponent of the West.

This ban is even more awkward because of the depiction of the communists in the film. They are the man victims in the movie which are killed by a 'Nazi' and had to pay with their lives because of their resistance. In contrast to that is the position of the rich ship-owner who belongs to the upper class respectively the

[35] Ibid, unpaginated.
[36] Ibid, unpaginated.

Bourgeoisie and helps to kill the communists. This emphasizes that the capitalist had supported the Nazi regime and points therefore indirectly to the FRG and its system. Thus the 'anti-Fascist' position of the GDR is underlined and strengthened again.

Furthermore the characters of the communists are mostly brave and bolt men, who accept their destinies. One could say they are shown like martyrs who bear the ordeals of the Nazis. Thus this film also contains role models of communists, as in *Rotation* and *The Council of Gods* to make the viewer aware of the 'good' communists fighting against the 'evil' Nazi regime.[37]

3.5 The Kaiser's Lackey (1951)

The second important Staudte film deals with German nationalism and its impact on the people in the Wilhemine Germany. It bases on Heinrich Mann's novel 'Der Untertan' from 1918 and clearly shows how militaristic, national and authoritarian traditions led to World War I.

Diedrich Heßling is a very weak and insecure little boy, because he is frightened by his father, mother, etc. When he gets older he learns how to push through his own ideas and wishes. From then on his motto is "bow to those at the top and tread on those below"[38]. By keeping this motto he succeeds in school, in the university, in his fraternity and when he gets the owner of the family paper factory. He also goes into politics to follow his beloved emperor William II. Therefore he holds a speech in his hometown when a statue of William II. is built there. During

---

[37] DEFA Film Library at the University of Massachusetts Amherst, "Rotation", unpaginated.
[38] DEFA Film Library at the University of Massachusetts Amherst, "Der Untertan (The Subject, or: The Kaiser's Lackey)" [http://www.umass.edu/defa/films/untertan.shtml] October 22, 2009, unpaginated.

his enthusiastic speech it starts heavily to rain and the scene fades into a destroyed city. [39]

As *The Axe of Wandsbek* this movie was also banned, but this time in West Germany[40] because the West German officials concluded that this film is a role model for communist ideology. All around the world the film became very successful and was not banned at all which illustrates that the FRG officials also tried to diminish communist influence among international politics respectively weaken the ideological opponent.

Taking the U.S. critique into consideration one recognizes some propagandistic issues within the film. First of all the relationship between Heßling and his workers in the factory is a good example. He is depicted as a cruel and hard factory owner who only wants to make profit and does not really care about the fate of his workers. This obviously mirrors the communist view of the working class people and the bourgeoisie and that the latter ones always make their profit by misusing their workers. Nevertheless one has to say that this relationship between Heßling and his workers is not at the center of the movie because the relationship is rarely shown in the film.

Much more interesting is the depiction of the character of Napoleon Fischer, who is a socialist worker in the factory of Heßling. According to Susanne Brandt the character was shown friendlier than in the novel of Heinrich Mann.[41] This emphasizes that the communist film maker respectively the GDR regime were

---

[39] Ibid, unpaginated.
[40] Susanne Brandt, "Geschichte und Film", 9.
[41] Ibid, 7.

interested in showing a socialist character as a contrast to the powerful Heßling and that the viewer sees that the socialist were the ones who fought for their comrades in the factories and also fought against a too powerful bourgeoisie in the Wilhelmine Germany. Furthermore Napoleon Fischer mirrors the always occurring socialist person which also can be found in the other films described above.

Nevertheless GDR friendly officials also criticized the film for showing the working class to less.[42] This apparently underlines that the film was not as much influenced by the GDR regime as others before and makes the FRG ban somehow illogical.

3.6 Naked Among Wolves (1963)

The movie deals with concentration camp inmates hiding a Jewish baby what endangers the planned liberation of the Buchenwald concentration camp through them and the closing U.S. Army. The film was directed by Frank Beyer and is based on the book of the same title, written by Bruno Apitz in 1958.[43]

The Buchenwald concentration camp during the last days of World War II: Every day new fleeing prisoners of Auschwitz arrive at the camp. One of them is the Jew Jankowski who carries a huge piece of luggage with him. In this case he hides a Jewish child which is detected by members of the international camp Committee which plans a resistance action against the camp guards to free themselves. The leaders of the committee argue if they should keep the child within the camp or should release it with Jankowski. Finally the child stays in the camp but

---

[42] Ibid, 8.
[43] DEFA Film Library at the University of Massachusetts Amherst, "Nackt unter Wölfen (Naked Among Wolves)" [http://www.umass.edu/defa/filmtour/sjwolves.shtml] October 22, 2009, unpaginated.

18

is detected by a SS guard and therefore some leaders of the resistance committee are arrested, tortured and killed. The camp guards cannot agree on how to deal with the rest of the prisoners because some want to kill them all following the Nazi doctrine while others prefer to save them and get less punished by the closing allies. Because of these differences between the camp guards the resistance group can hide the baby and finally organize the liberation of the camp.[44]

Nearly 20 years after the end of World War II this was the first GDR film that dealt with concentration camps. Interestingly not the Jews but rather the (socialist) resistance group was in the focus of that movie. Thomas Fox confirms that by saying that Naked among Wolves "provides a paradigmatic example of anti-Semitism as a peripheral phenomenon, one subordinate to class struggle"[45]. Thus it is very obvious that the GDR regime used this film to spread its propaganda and ideology instead of dealing with the Holocaust and the Jewish life in concentration camps in a serious and reasonable way. Therefore the viewer is betrayed by watching the movie because he or she could assume that the film deals with the topics concentration camp and Nazi Past and therefore underlines the GDR's position as an 'anti-Fascist' state. But by mainly focusing on the communist resistance, the film makers just use the setting of the concentration camp to hide the ideological propaganda of the GDR and therefore the film cannot be seen as a serious-meant movie of an 'anti-Fascist' state.[46]

---

[44] David Scrase, "Naked among Wolves (Nackt unter Wölfen)" [http://www.novelguide.com/a/disc over/rghl_01/rghl_01_00424.html] October 22, 2009, unpaginated.
[45] Thomas Fox, *Stated Memory: East Germany and the Holocaust* (Rochester, NY: Camden House, 1999), 103-104.
[46] David Scrase, "Naked among Wolves", unpaginated.

Furthermore the communists are depicted as the life savers of Jews who always would help the poor and neglected. Additionally they also bear the ordeals of torture and death to protect the Jews. That makes the GDR viewer proud of being a member of a communist state and therefore the regime could strengthen its position. So the film makers legitimize the GDR's statues of an 'antifascist' again.

All in all one can say that this movie is another example of films which were produced in favor of the GDR regime. Although it was made in the early 1960's, a time when some GDR film makers created system-critical movies, the officials continued using films as a means of propaganda and to promote communism. Particularly in difficult times for the regime, e.g. after the building of the wall in 1961, films like Naked among Wolves naturally helped to regain confidence of the population.

3.7 Carbide and Sorrel (1965)

Another Frank Beyer film was *Carbide and Sorrel* which is set in the immediate postwar Germany and deals satirically with the political instable situation, the destroyed infrastructure of East Germany as well as life in the Soviet occupation zone. [47]

After the end of the Second World War the worker Karl Blücher, called Kalle, has to go from Dresden to Wittenberg to get Carbide from his brother-in-law because he and his colleagues want to build up a cigarette factory again. Once he gets the seven barrels of carbide his journey back to Dresden seems like an

---

[47] Karen Kramer, "Karbid und Sauerampfer (Carbide and Sorrel)" [http://www.umass.edu/defa/films/karbid_und_sauerampfer.shtml] October 22, 2009, unpaginated.

adventure. At first he meets the young peasant Karla, with whom he falls in love. But before starting a relationship with her he wants to bring back the carbide. On his way he gets arrested by the Red Army because they want to have the carbide as a tax. Furthermore Kalle gets to know other persons as the opera singer, Ms. Clara Himmel and an American officer. When he finally arrives at Dresden he has only two barrels of carbide left. After that he leaves Dresden and goes back to his love Karla.[48]

After the erection of the wall in 1961 the GDR filmmakers hoped and thought to have the possibilities to deal with sociopolitical problems in their films because the country was even more isolated from the West and the regime would also allow system critical scenes in films respectively reduce ideological propaganda in DEFA films. Nevertheless this regime critical film period did not last for long because as said before the regime banned lots of films in 1965. The movie *Carbide and Sorrel* could only be published because it was finished before the ban.[49]

Therefore Beyer used the chance to show some GDR critical issues within his movie, but covers it up by using satirical means. For example the issue of a cigarette factory was certainly not that kind of factory that the communist leaders think of because cigarettes are not so important to establish socialism. Moreover Kalle is not depicted as a socialist hero who wants to reestablish a factory as soon as possible. Instead his journey back to Dresden seems really relaxed and he is not too eager to get back as quick as possible. So it emphasizes that Beyer did not want to make the film too heroic or depict Kalle as a role model of communism.

---

[48] Ibid, unpaginated.
[49] Ibid, unpaginated.

Furthermore Kalle also plays around with the Soviet Army officers. When he gets caught a second time he just gave them a barrel of chalk instead of carbide as tax. Thus illustrates that the movie makes somehow fun of the Red Army and depicts them kind of stupid. Thus all of the points make obvious that the director tried to make a less ideological film but show the situation after World War II from a more neutral and clear viewpoint.[50]

Nevertheless the movie also contains some regime supporting scenes. The most striking one is certainly Kalle's meeting with the U.S. officer. When he is stranded the American comes closer with a speedboat. Additionally this is underlined by a really triumphant music which should illustrate the U.S. advancements of modern technology. But when Kalle wins the boat over to transport his carbide he leaves behind the U.S. soldier. This makes the viewer believe that despite the modern Western technology the East is still smart enough to oppose it. Furthermore the officer is depicted in an uglier way than the Soviet soldiers, e.g. through is evil facial expressions and the officer calls Kalle a Nazi when he wins the boat over. Therefore the viewer should think that the U.S. people as well as other capitalists are very cruel and bad persons. Additionally the U.S. officers are illustrated as people who still see all Germans as Nazis which puts a negative sight on the U.S. memory of Nazism. Last but not least Kalle also makes fun of the U.S. officers who stand ashore because he passes them with the speedboat and beckons them. He is not detected because he wears the hat of the U.S. officer he got the boat from. This implies that the viewer could think that the East Germans (and their

---

[50] Ibid, unpaginated.

ideology) are smarter as the West Germans respectively capitalist Americans. Another example is the scene where Kalle eats an American 'Spearmint' bubble gum and calls it weird food. So this can be seen as an attack on American food and the Western countries which consumed it.

All in all, these scenes obviously show that GDR film makers also incorporated communist ideologies in their films in the time period between the building of the wall and 1965.

3.8 The Gleiwitz Case (1961)

Shortly after the building of the wall in 1961 the film of Gerhard Klein was published. The film deals with the faked Nazi attack on Gleiwitz radio station which was close to the Polish border. The attack was used to legitimate a Nazi attack on Poland which was eventually the beginning of World War II.

In the night of August 31 to September 1, 1939 SS head storm leader Naujoks, was in charge of the operation. Polish-speaking ethnic Germans from an SS fencing academy acted as the Polish attackers, and a German concentration camp prisoner, clad in a Polish uniform, was left shot at the radio station as an evidence of the Polish attack.[51]

Although the film was published shortly after the building of the wall, it can be seen as one of the least influenced movies by the GDR regime. "Ein Film über die Möglichkeiten und Techniken von Provokationen, der Manipulierung von

---

[51] Sabine Hake, "The Gleiwitz Case (Der Fall Gleiwitz)" [http://www.umass.edu/defa/moma2.sht ml] October 22, 2009, unpaginated.

Tatsachen und Meinungen, ein Film, der absolut im Trend der Zeit [...] und mit dieser Intention auch erdacht wurde."[52]

Therefore the film can be seen as the role model of the period between the building of the wall and 1965, when GDR film makers tended to be more system critical by using complex topics and more innovative and interesting technical means within their movies. Above all the technical means make the film perfectly fit into this time period.

Firstly, the film seems like a documentary because the scenes are chronologically ordered and give an overview of the Gleiwitz case without any ideological implications. Thus the film maker really focuses on a neutral historical account of the events in 1939.[53]

Secondly, "the carefully composed shots of ordinary settings and locations, the hard lighting and low camera angles in the close-ups of faces and the preference for geometrical configurations in the exterior scenes"[54] can be compared to films of Nazi film maker Leni Riefenstahl.[55]

Naturally this cinematic style was not likely seen by the GDR regime and accused the film makers of celebrating Nazism and therefore offending the communist state and its status as an 'anti-Fascist' state. Because of that the film only lasted a few weeks in the cinema and was also banned from the Moscow International Film festival in 1961.[56]

---

[52] DVD.de, "Der Fall Gleiwitz (DVD)" [http://datenbank.dvd.de/film/der-fall-gleiwitz-dvd] October 22, 2009, unpaginated.
[53] Sabine Hake, "The Gleiwitz Case", unpaginated.
[54] Ibid, unpaginated.
[55] Ibid, unpaginated,
[56] Ibid, unpaginated.

Surprisingly the movie was not banned from the GDR regime from the beginning. Maybe the official did not want to appear as dictators who want to ban everything opposing the regime right after building of the wall. The situation could have become more instable within the country because the people could have felt restricted more and more. Thus the regime probably waited a few weeks to take it out rather unnoticed by the population. The reactions of the GDR and Soviet officials make clear that the influence of propaganda in films was still evaluated as very important and inevitable for the country and therefore the ban of further critical films against the regime was just a question of time.

3.9 I Was Nineteen (1968)

The film is based on the director's (Konrad Wolf) memoirs of his time as a lieutenant in the Red Army in World War II and deals with a young boy who was born in Germany but serves in the Red Army during the last days of World War II.[57]

His name is Gregor Hecker, who was originally born in Germany but grew up in Russia and therefore serves for the Red Army in the Second World War. When he enters Germany he becomes lieutenant and works as a translator for the Russians. That is the reason why he is sometimes mistaken as a German soldier from the Soviets but also gets in trouble with the German soldiers. Finally he and his Russian comrades save some German deserters and bring them back to the Soviet Union as P.O.W.[58]

---

[57] Stuart Henderson, "I was nineteen" [http://www.popmatters.com/pm/review/i-was-nineteen] October 22, 2009, unpaginated.
[58] Ibid, unpaginated.

This very personal film of Konrad Wolf is a rather different war movie compared to the usual type of this genre. Combat scenes as well as a heroic depiction of a soldier are not in the centre of this movie but the illustration of the young soldier and his personal conflict of invading his own home country. This emphasizes that the director wants the young people of his generation make aware of the topic and wants to make them feel with the young soldier.

Furthermore the personal conflict of the soldier also emphasizes a conflict of personal identity as well as national identity. A topic which was certainly interesting for young people in the GDR in the 1960's after the erection of the wall and further events. So the author wants to make the viewer think about his own nationality and maybe tries to strengthen a national GDR identity within the viewer. Naturally, this identity issue was likely seen by the GDR regime which needed any form of support after 1961 to strengthen its position against Western Germany and in international politics.[59]

Nevertheless, the GDR regime criticized Wolf that his movie did not provide strongly enough the political message as well as he illustrates the German soldier in a nice way whereas the Soviet soldiers were displayed as harsh and somehow dangerous what becomes obvious when the girl asks Gregor to protect her from the Russian soldiers.[60]

---

[59] Marc Silberman, "German Cinema", page 158-160.
[60] Ibid, 160.

This clearly shows that the regime was seldom completely satisfied with the films in terms of ideology and politics and therefore tried a lot to make them fit as best as possible to the ideology of the country, which underlines its importance and the regimes legitimacy.

4. Conclusion

With regard to the role(s) of the memory of the Nazi Past and the Holocaust in the German Democratic Republic Films it was illustrated that the Nazi Past played an important role in the memory of World War II in the German Democratic Republic. Especially the crimes and cruelties of the Nazis were highly discussed. The memory of the Holocaust respectively the role of the Jews in World War II was rather neglected despite some obvious similarities between the communists of the Soviet Union and the Jews concerning the suffering and the ordeals during World War II. The marginalization of the Jews was not a case for the FRG officials what implied first Cold War conflicts within the memory of the Nazi Past.

Furthermore it could be proved that the GDR regime used the films as a means of propaganda and could therefore spread its ideology among the film viewers. That was more and more strengthened as the Cold War got more and more intense.

This could be shown by the movies *The Blum Affair*, *Rotation*, *The Kaiser's Lackey* and especially in the movies *The Council of Gods* as well as *The Axt of Wandsbek*. The overall topic of all these movies was the question of guilt concerning the Nazi Past and was used to glorify and to promote the communist resistance.

Similarly to the developments in the GDR in the early 1960's the movies became more critical towards the regime. Especially new techniques and more complex stories were a new way to make less propagandistic films. *The Gleiwitz Case* as well as *Carbide and Sorrel* are typical examples of these new forms of films. After the flood of banned GDR film productions by the regime in 1965 the film makers focused more on less controversial movies like *I was nineteen*. Nevertheless one has to say that the influence and the propaganda of the regime was not that obvious in the movies of the 1960's as at the beginning of the GDR in the early 1950's. Although the regime never gave up its influence in films and the 1960's films also contained regime propaganda, the emergent system critical movies of this decade can be seen as the beginning of a less effective influence of the regime in film productions as well as in other aspects of life.

5. Bibliography

Berghan, Daniela. *Hollywood behind the Wall: The cinema of East Germany* [http://books.google.com/books?id=JAr2pv4R6kIC&printsec=frontcover&dq=holl ywood+behind+the+wall&hl=de&cd=1#v=onepage&q=&f=false] December 1, 2009.

Susanne Brandt, *Geschichte und Film: Der Untertan (1951)* [www.phil-fak.uni-duesseldorf.de/.../Der_Untertan_Geschichte_und_Film__kurz_.pdf] December 1, 2009.

Buening, Michael. *Cautionary Tales* [http://www.popmatters.com/pm/review/council-of-the-gods-der-rat-der-g/] October 22, 2009.

DEFA Film Library at the University of Massachusetts Amherst. *Affaire Blum (The Blum Affair)* [http://www.umass.edu/defa/filmtour/sjblum.shtml] October 22, 2009.

DEFA Film Library at the University of Massachusetts Amherst. *Das Beil von Wandsbek (The Axt of Wandsbek)* [http://www.umass.edu/defa/filmtour/sjaxe.shtml] October 22, 2009.

DEFA Film Library at the University of Massachusetts Amherst, *Der Untertan (The Subject, or: The Kaiser's Lackey)* [http://www.umass.edu/defa/films/untertan.shtml] October 22, 2009.

DEFA Film Library at the University of Massachusetts Amherst. *Nackt unter Wölfen (Naked Among Wolves)* [http://www.umass.edu/defa/filmtour/sjwolves.shtml] October 22, 2009.

DEFA Film Library at the University of Massachusetts Amherst. *Rat der Götter (Council of Gods* [http://www.umass.edu/defa/filmtour/sjrat.shtml] October 22, 2009.

DEFA Film Library at the University of Massachusetts Amherst. *Rotation* [http://www.umass.edu/defa/filmtour/sjrotation.shtml] October 22, 2009.

DVD.de. *Der Fall Gleiwitz (DVD)* [http://datenbank.dvd.de/film/der-fall-gleiwitz-dvd] October 22, 2009.

Finker, Kurt. *Zwischen Integration und Legitimation: Der antifaschistische Widerstandskampf in Geschichtsbild und Geschichtsschreibung der DDR.* Schkeuditz: GNN Verlag, 1999.

Fox, Thomas. *Stated Memory: East Germany and the Holocaust.* Rochester, NY: Camden House, 1999.

Hake, Sabine. *The Gleiwitz Case (Der Fall Gleiwitz)* [http://www.umass.edu/defa/moma2.shtml] October 22, 2009.

Henderson, Stuart. *I was nineteen* [http://www.popmatters.com/pm/review/i-was-nineteen] October 22, 2009.

Herf, Jeffrey. *Divided Memory: The Nazi Past in the Two Germanys.* Cambridge, MA: Harvard University Press, 1997.

Kramer, Karen. *Karbid und Sauerampfer (Carbide and Sorrel)* [http://www.umass.edu/defa/films/karbid_und_sauerampfer.shtml] October 22, 2009.

Mückenberger, Christiane. "The Anti-Fascist Past in DEFA Films" in *DEFA: East German Cinema 1946-1992*, ed. Seán Allan and John Sandford, 58-76. [http://books.google.com/books?id=3xDwYDJlklkC&printsec=frontcover&dq=DEFA&hl=de&cd=1#v=onepage&q=&f=false] December 1, 2009.

Scrase, David. *Naked among Wolves (Nackt unter Wölfen)* [http://www.novelguide.com/a/discover/rghl_01/rghl_01_00424.html] October 22, 2009.

Silberman, Marc. *German Cinema: Texts in Context* [http://books.google.com/books?id=xzfbyafOb4QC&printsec=frontcover&dq=German+cinema&hl=de&cd=2#v=onepage&q=&f=false] December 1, 2009.